T0011105

STRIKERS
and
SCARVES
Behind the Scenes
of Match Day Soccer

by Thomas Kingsley Troupe

CAPSTONE PRESS
a capstone imprint

Published by Spark, an imprint of Capstone
1710 Roe Crest Drive, North Mankato, Minnesota 56003
capstonepub.com

Copyright © 2023 by Spark. All rights reserved. No part of this publication may be reproduced in whole or in part, or stored in a retrieval system, or transmitted in any form or by any means, electronic, mechanical, photocopying, recording, or otherwise, without written permission of the publisher.

Library of Congress Cataloging-in-Publication Data is available on the Library of Congress website.

ISBN: 9781669003397 (hardcover)
ISBN: 9781669040354 (paperback)
ISBN: 9781669003359 (ebook PDF)

Summary: Think a soccer match begins with the opening kickoff? Think again! In this Sports Illustrated Kids book, go behind the scenes of a typical match day in professional soccer—from prepping the pitch and cleaning cleats to player escorts and jersey swaps. This fast-paced, fact-filled book will give soccer fans, young and old, a brand-new perspective on major league soccer.

Editor: Donald Lemke; Designer: Tracy Davies; Media Researcher: Svetlana Zhurkin; Production Specialist: Katy LaVigne

Image Credits
Associated Press: dpa/picture-alliance/Michael Deines, 16, Icon Sportswire, 23, Michael Probst, 19; Getty Images: AFP/Franck Fife, 17, Alex Broadway, 18, Alex Livesey, 8, Alex Morton, 11, Clive Mason, 12, Emilee Chinn, 4, George Wood, 7, Laurence Griffiths, 14, 20, Lionel Ng, 24, majorosl, 6, Mike Hewitt, 10, Naomi Baker, 27, Pool/Axel Heimken, 15, Pool/Carl Recine, 21, Pool/Julio Munoz, 9, Shaun Botterill, 26; Shutterstock: alphaspirit, cover (bottom left), Arina P. Habich, 29 (back), Damix, cover (bottom right), Di-mon, 29 (top), Dziurek, 5, Gyuszko-Photo, cover (bottom middle), irin-k, cover (top right), 1, littlewoody, 13, Paolo Bona, 22, Ron Dale (background), cover, back cover, Vasyl Shulga, cover (top); Sports Illustrated: Erick W. Rasco, 25

All internet sites appearing in back matter were available and accurate when this book was sent to press.

TABLE OF CONTENTS

Words in **bold** are in the glossary.

IT'S SOCCER TIME

The crowd roars as the ball rockets downfield. The striker controls the ball, moving through defenders. In scoring range, they line up a kick and . . . GOAL!

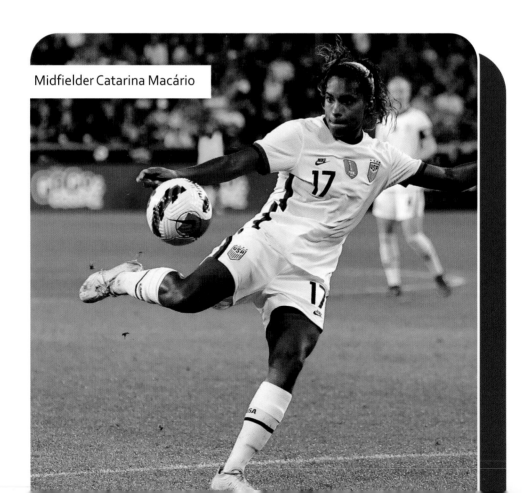
Midfielder Catarina Macário

Members of the Chilean soccer team celebrate after a goal.

Professional soccer matches are exciting. A lot of people work hard to bring these fast-paced events to life. Tighten your **cleats**! It's match day for soccer!

PITCH PREP

There is no soccer match without the field, or pitch. Groundskeepers maintain the grass at indoor and outdoor **stadiums**. They make sure the grass is cut and rolled.

A cover protects the grass at Elland Road stadium in Leed, England.

Grass shouldn't be taller than .8–1.36 inches (20–35 millimeters). The right length allows soccer balls to move at faster speeds. Covers help keep the grass from freezing.

FACT

In many countries around the world, a soccer field is called a pitch. The British definition of pitch is "a playing field."

7

The lines on a soccer field are painted weekly during the season. For pro matches, they are often given two coats. It helps the lines stand out.

Soccer goals are an important part of the game. The net is attached to the goalposts and crossbar. Worn nets are quickly replaced.

Staff fix the net at La Cartuja Stadium in Seville, Spain.

FAN EXPERIENCE

One of the biggest parts of a soccer match is the fans. People pack stadiums to watch their favorite teams. Ticket booths sell tickets to the games.

Vendors keep hungry and thirsty fans happy. Some sell items right in the stands. This lets fans keep their eyes on the match.

FACT

Soccer is easily the most popular sport on Earth. There are about 3.5 billion soccer fans worldwide!

Soccer fans are serious about their sport. Many dress in jerseys, wave team scarves, or even paint their faces. They cheer their teams to victory.

Most soccer stadiums have stores to sell **souvenirs** to fans. The shopkeepers make sure to have enough items to sell before and after the match.

HIGH TECH

To bring fans closer to the game, soccer stadiums rely on **technology**. Scoreboards display the score and time left. Some have built-in screens for fans to see the action up close.

Stadium **technicians** check to make sure everything works like it should. They will make repairs when needed before the big match.

A public address, or PA, system helps fans know what's happening on the field. It allows **announcers** to speak to the crowd.

Workers perform system checks before every match. Sound technicians want to make sure the sound is crisp, clear, and loud enough.

Not everyone can see the game in person. Camera crews capture the game so viewers can cheer on their team from home. They set up many cameras and test their equipment before kickoff.

Because soccer is loved worldwide, broadcasters send their video to **satellites**. From there, the soccer match is sent to TVs and computers everywhere.

On the field, referees make sure everything is ready for the match. They check that the soccer balls are inflated to the right size. The referees also check the nets and field.

If a referee sees any reason the match shouldn't start, they can **postpone** or cancel it.

FACT ///////////////////////////

The main referee in a soccer match can run as much or more than the players do. They average about 6–8 miles (9.7–12.9 kilometers) per match!

Soccer fans can get excited! A security team makes sure everyone is following the rules off the field. They look for any signs of trouble.

In the locker room, players from both teams get ready. They put on their uniforms and gear. They listen to their coaches.

D.C. United locker room

GAME ON!

When everything is ready to go, the gates to the stadium open. Tickets are sold. Fans buy food and drinks. They find their way to their seats.

Players for the U.S. Women's national soccer team pose with young fans before a game.

The players from each team make their way through the tunnel to the field. Sometimes the players are joined by children. It's almost time for kickoff!

FACT

Child escorts have been a tradition in soccer for more than 20 years. The escorts were thought to raise awareness for charity causes. They also remind fans to help make the world a place "fit for children."

A lot happens behind the scenes in a soccer stadium. There are countless people working hard to make sure everything is ready.

Star soccer player Cristiano Ronaldo

Fans mostly focus on the star players on the field. But before an athlete makes the first kick, hundreds of stars make sure that match day happens!

PLAN YOUR MATCH DAY

Want to have your own match day? Be a behind-the-scenes star at your own stadium—right at home. Here are some things you can do to make it happen!

- Design your own tickets and give them to your friends and family.

- Prepare lots of snacks. Try something healthy along with the usual stadium treats.

- Decorate with pennants and team colors. Make signs for your friends to wave around during the match.

- Have guests sit in the "press box" and give commentary on the action happening on the field.

- Create a wacky dance and cheer that you and your friends can do when your team scores. Be sure to yell "GOOOOOOOOOOAL" whenever the ball makes it into the net!

GLOSSARY

announcer (uh-NOWN-sur)—a person who describes and comments on the action in a broadcast sports event

cleats (KLEETS)—shoes equipped with plastic or metal spikes or projects on the soles to provide traction

postpone (post-POHN)—put off an event until a later time

satellite (SAT-uh-lyte)—a man-made object or vehicle intended to orbit the earth

souvenir (SOO-vuh-neer)—something that serves as a reminder

stadium (STAY-dee-uhm)—a large, usually roofless, building with rows of seats for spectators at modern sports events

technician (tek-NISH-uhn)—a specialist in the technical details of a subject

technology (tek-NAHL-uh-gee)—the use of science in solving problems

vendor (VEN-duhr)—one that sells something

READ MORE

Abdo, Kenny. *History of Soccer.* Mankato, MN: ABDO Publishing, 2020.

Greder, Andy. *Behind the Scenes Soccer.* Minneapolis: Lerner Publishing, 2020.

Terrell, Brandon. *Game Day Soccer: An Interactive Sports Story.* North Mankato, MN: Capstone, 2021.

INTERNET SITES

DK Findout!: Soccer
dkfindout.com/us/sports/soccer/

Kids-Play-Soccer: Basic Soccer Rules
kids-play-soccer.com/basic-soccer-rules.html

Sports Illustrated Kids: Soccer
sikids.com/tag/soccer

INDEX

ABOUT THE AUTHOR

Thomas Kingsley Troupe is the author of a big ol' pile of books for kids. He's written about everything from ghosts to Bigfoot to 3rd grade werewolves. He even wrote a book about dirt. When he's not writing or reading, he investigates the strange and spooky as part of the Twin Cities Paranormal Society. Thomas lives in Woodbury, Minnesota, with his two sons.